Sucking at Sti

Emily Hinshelwood was
1967. She was educated a   ...u
London Universities and w   ...u for ten years as a
development anthropologist. Now she is a freelance
writer, performer and workshop facilitator and lives
in South Wales.

EMILY HINSHELWOOD

Sucking at Sticky Fingers

For Sue,
Best wishes
Emily x

R
P Roynetree
Press

Published in 2004 by
Roynetree Press
Pant yr Ywen, Llwyncelyn Road
Tai'rgwaith, Ammanford
SA18 1UU

A CIP Record for this book is available from the
British Cataloguing in Publication Data Office

ISBN 0-9548149-0-8

Printed by Gwasg Dinefwr Press Ltd., Llandybie,
Carmarthenshire

www.emily-hinshelwood.co.uk

for dan

Acknowledgements

I would like to thank the following publications in which several poems in this collection have appeared in some form: *Red Poets* ('A Silence', 'Gene Genie', 'No More Old Maid', 'Coke'), *Roundyhouse* ('Techno-trouble', 'For a Cuddle', 'Instant Satisfaction for 99p'), *Athena* ('Bills and Moon'), *Permanent Waves* ('The Scrap', 'Coke'). 'Ultimate Act of Love', 'Catching Fish in Swansea Bay' and 'Which God?' have also appeared on the Welsh Academy website.

I would also like to thank the following friends and family: Anna Smith, Marion Preece, Hillary Wickers, Gerrie Hughes, Ron Meldon, Michael Marriott, Sarah Savage and Dan McCallum for their constructive criticism and invaluable feedback; Elin McCallum and Eva Weinmayr for their artistic input; PennyAnne Windsor, Derek Cobley and Maggie Trevett-Evans for their consistent support for my writing; and my family and friends for their love.

Contents

Blood Orange and Crystallised Ginger

Blueprints

I scour the dusty drawer for blueprints
musty pages beiged over centuries
crumpled, wrinkled, DNAed instructions
of who or what I ought to be.

I rifle through files of famous figures
pegged as models for all to admire
to aspire to assimilate
perpetuating roles,
exacerbating crises of identity.

I glance over genetic investigations
skim-read science's speculations
of why I should do and where I should be.

But after wading through mottled papers,
stats, snaps, manuals, graphs
the drawer is bare.
Just a cobweb over there
a dried raisin, a tired elastic band
comb with a stray strand of hair.

There are no blueprints,
no diagrams or step-by-step instructions
for installing the flat-pack human being.

The drawer is empty, the page is clean.
I take a pencil and design my very own
tailor-made
me.

honeyed milk & brandy cream

The Transit of Venus

As I rambled through Glanaman just the other day
the radio related the latest research:
'nine out of ten women prefer men who read books'.
It's no longer looks that count
no more the hunt for a man who can cook
no, what hooks the girl
is the nose in the book
and size does *not* matter.

Well – on I went down the Amman
and news of the research had arrived in the town
it was ramshackle, topsy-turvy turned completely
upside down
and quiet as an ancient text.

Men on every corner idling with a book
semi-clad lads outside 'Harrods'
reading *Sense and Sensibility*
cocking their eyebrows seductively.

Chekhov at the check-out in the co-op
Lolita loitering in the aisles
Trollope propped on trolleys down at Tesco's
Dickens among the chickens
and outside 'Shoppers' World'
was a suave stallion
sporting the *Complete Works of Shakespeare*
upside down.

Hands bookshop had cleared its stock

the queue for the library went three times round the
block
with blokes of every age
itching to get a feel of the words on the page
a taste of the stories, a scent of the plot
to dip their sticky fingers in the literature pot.

I stopped and gazed, amazed
like every other woman that day
rooted to the spot
aroused and hot at the sight
of such a *sensitive* lot.

And women flocked to gawp and stare
to giggle and flirt
touching the hems of their skimpy skirts
mad with desire, on fire and
soon the town erupted in a frenzy
of sensuality
like writhing snakes in a steaming bed
with just one thing in everybody's head.

And up in the skies above
was the face of Venus, the goddess of love
passing across the sun
plucking the heartstrings of everyone.

And if, through special spectacles,
you were to look
you'd notice that Venus
was reading a book.

Firstborn

It was you
who turned me into a parent.

From the moment they cut the cord
I became the Milk Marketing Board
twenty-four hour emergency services
minister for education, recreation
on-call night and day.

It was you
who helped me see
what it is simply to 'be':
how smiles erupt
how fingers grow
strangers' faces you start to know
how noises turn to speech.
It was you
who taught me how to teach.

Above all else you found in me
a love I'd never felt –
dealt like a wild card.

I had searched the world
for the meaning of life:
when you were born
I knew

it was you.

How do I love you? Let me count the ways

after Elizabeth Barratt Browning's poem of the same
name

for dan

I love you to the ocean's final drip
the last candescent snuffle of the sun;
the blizzard that exhausted everyone
and blew the course of each surviving ship.
I love you like a skittish monkey's skip
a writhing knot of smugglers on the run
the highly charged desires of a nun
the spark and lightning of a cracking whip.
I love you for the passion in your heart
your humour and your ever-present cheer
and though I loved you almost from the start
I cannot help but love you more each year;
and even if death forces us apart
my love for you will never disappear.

Catching Fish in Swansea Bay

Sixty years ago today
the village had a trip to Swansea Bay.
I was too young to go without Mam
just Billy could go on the trip for the day.

I'll catch for you, he said
the biggest fish in Swansea Bay
I'll hold it at the window
so be sure to meet the train

and they crowded on the platform on that hot, sunny
day:
Mr Morgan with his black box camera
Mrs Phillips with her baby dressed in lace
the minister rallying the Sunday school
chasing and racing all over the place.

I whiled away that lonely day
till I heard
not far away
clashing of steel, grinding of wheel.
I ran through the night – feet flying fast
to see if the biggest
ever
fish was going passed.

The great train hissed to a grinding halt.
And out of the grey,
a single cornet started to play.

No cheering,
no laughter,
no song.

Doors opened slowly to the cornet's refrain.
Tearstained cheeks stepped down from the train.

Mr Morgan with his head hung low
Mrs Phillips clutched her baby very tight
the minister handed down each child.

All the while the cornet played I waited for Billy
who never came.

If you ask people now they always say,
he's catching fish in Swansea Bay.

For a Cuddle

Your eyelids heavy.
Long lashes
lips parted
breathing a deep
steady rhythm of dreams.

A faint noise escapes your lips.
Your hair against the pillow
arms outstretched.
Teddy bear abandoned.

You came into my bed
in the middle of the night.
For a cuddle.

I love that.
You creep to my room
and hover by the bed
waiting
for me to lift the covers
and draw you in for a cuddle.

And if I'm feeling sad
or scared
in the middle of the night
could I creep into your room
and hover?

Could I crawl in beside you
for a cuddle?

Suleimaniya

Above the mountain of Asmar
Venus watched
and reeled off a round from her kalashnikov
no delicate arrow from Cupid's bow
no
the goddess of love dealt a mighty blow
blasting bullets from a BKC
laying landmines on every boundary
piling ordnance for a frenzy
of fireworks

wham bam thank-you Saddam
sharing honey in a hot hammam
pomegranates, guavas, kiwis, limes,
goblin market, *alekum asalam*

armed peshmerga to guard the passion
rocking in a ricochet of Iraqi friction
reeling from that kiss
in almond-scented bliss.

Venus smiled
her work done
she blew the smoke from the end of her gun,
and gave the thumbs-up sign to everyone

for out of the carnage
and the dust in the sky
there rose a love that will never
ever die.

Riding the *Seventh Wave*

Your thin chest sucks shallow breaths.
Dark curls haphazard in the sun's pool
on this
hated bed.

Eyes flicker.
A dream on yellow rays,
plays behind your pale lids.
A dream of what could be.

There is music in your head
castanets, stamping feet.
Silk, feathers
in sweating heat.

But each day your hunger fades
your eyes retreat to milky skies
where clouds obscure
our whispered plans
of tiny feet
nurtured
by a three-course life of love.

You shall not slip away.
Tonight we shall ride
the *Seventh Wave*.

We'll toast fresh crab by midnight's cove
seduced by the tune of the fireflies' spark
and dressed in silken reds

with fingers clacking the castanets
rosettes of jasmine in our hair
we'll dance
to music from the mountain air.

Hands held high
we'll lift our jangling feet
in time to the thieving, feverish beat.

And together
you and me
we'll dance into the deep bass yearning of the sea.
We'll dance to our grave
tonight,
we'll ride the *Seventh Wave.*

Ultimate Act of Love

A ragged moon shivers.
You lie
like a fading ghost
shrunken, shrivelled - a crumpled shadow

drugged and dragged from dignity
in shallow breaths and morphined silence.

Hands that rocked me
hang like dried-out sticks.
Tongue that sang lullabies
now lolls from a wordless hole.
Warm eyes are lost in a milky white sea

yet still
they won't set you free.

Like a kite in a full-bellied wind
they tug and pull and yank with the string of
Hippocrates.
Needles-tubes-bags-drips-beeping
semi-sleeping in starched
stained sheets.

And you lie –
 a slumped sack
heart rattling the bars of this
graceless
hell.

Pillow stuffed with death's soft feathers
firmly placed

I let you go.

Freedom oozes from your wrinkled body
picks up its heels and tickles the air
dancing light-footed on my words.

Cradle in your hands the cheeks of the sun.
Drink through your feet the gold in the cracks in the
rocks.
Billow your body with a whistling wind
and ride the crest of the breaking seas.

Looking for Love

I was sweet sixteen
I was all fired up
in me stockings and suspenders
I was looking for love
and I had a little cuddle
and a fiddle here and there
and I reaped a chain of love bites
and some gaudy underwear
but I wasn't disappointed
I was still fired up
it's a full time job this looking for love.

So I set about in earnest
with me rucksack all packed up
and I headed out the country
I was looking for love
and I shared a jug of ouzo
and a hammock made for two
I got asked to be married
I got asked for a screw
but I wasn't disappointed
I was still fired up
it's a full time job this looking for love.

At times I thought I'd found it
on the back-seat of a car
in a sweaty sultry jungle
in a bawdy backstreet bar
I'd pick it up and shake it
and examine it all round

but however much I looked
it was nowhere to be found.

I was in my twenties
hadn't found anyone
I'd given up on love
and I went looking for fun
I tried a bit of this
and I tried a bit of that
and with him or her or both of them
I'd rat a tat tat.

I wasn't disappointed
I was having a ball
I was frolicking and laughing
with no worries at all
I was young, free and single
I was all fired up
then without me even noticing...
along came love
and I wasn't disappointed
though I was a bit surprised
and I picked it up and shook it
and I looked it in the eyes
and sure enough before me
all fired up
stood the perfect example of full blown love.

We did a bit of this
and we did a bit of that
and forever more we frolicked
with a rat a tat tat.

First Year

Meet, talk, kiss, shag
kiss, shag, snog, shag
talk, shag, walk, shag
work, shag, snog, shag
work, walk, snog, shag
work, walk, talk, shag
snog, shag, snog, shag
shock at sprog…
                          shag
talk, shag, talk, shag
sleep, talk, sleep, shag
sleep, sleep, sleep, shag
buy big dress, shag
grow large breasts, shag
push and scream and
sprog comes quick and…

bleed, milk, leak, sag
milk, sleep, slog, sag
poo, sleep, milk, sag
milk, snog
            snog
                  sha….
milk, milk, sleep, sag
sleep, sag, sleep, sag
snog
      sleep
            snog
                  shhhhhhhhhag.

organic lime & fairtrade chocolate

A Silence

They took my dress when I came here
the cotton stained with yesterday's tear
and red
with the blood of my mother.

They took the bandage from my frostbitten feet
the dirty rag
a sheet
that belonged to my brother.

And in my head my memories fly
of Lhasa in flames, of dust in the sky
the policeman pulling my mother's hair
her mouth was screaming, her legs were bare.

They spoke to me in a foreign tongue
their eyeballs stared, their shouting stung
as they scribbled on their form.

Gave me water in a plastic beaker
issued vouchers for an asylum seeker
and stuck me in this children's dorm.

And in my mind my memories race
my burning home, my aunt's dead face
the escape I made up the mountainside
the shameful payment I made to the guide.

They took away my vanity
my dignity

my sanity.

But in my head my mind recalls
the wheels of prayer, the coloured shawls
my baby sister's laughing face
my mother's strength, my father's grace.

And though they say it'll damage my health,
I'll keep my memories to myself
because they are
as I can see
the one thing
they can't
take from me.

Weapons of Mass Destruction

Condoms are the stuff of mass destruction
according to inspectors from the United Nations.
So they sanction safe ejaculation
along with basic medication.

Condoms are the stuff of mass destruction
and are banned by Resolution
6159
no pleasuremax, playmix
extra fun or ultrafine
to enter the oil rich nation
that is getting ideas above its station.
No raised dots for greater sensation
no coloured, flavoured lubrication
or naked nuclear latex distraction
no uranium-loaded teat-ended action
and no Trojan *Supergun* spring spiral
for enhanced sexual satisfaction.

No stars and stripes G-ribbed
clitoral stimulation
and also
no basic medication.

No shoes, nappies, tampons, clothes
no ping pong balls, bog roll, toothpaste or biros
because
didn't you know
they are key to the production
of weapons of mass destruction.

Words from a Disgruntled Rat

*R*ats, rats, rats, they complain
dumping rubbish again and again.
They're dirty, they're vermin
they're ridden with fleas
they carry all kinds of disgusting disease.
They moan about us
they poison, they kill
yet continue to fill
and fill our land with rubbish.

Broken toys. Rusting cans.
Maggoty scraps. Smashed up vans.
Stinking nappies black with flies.
Rotting pets with rotting eyes.
Cattle slaughtered. Lambs diseased.
Batteries, paints and anti-freeze.

Hamburger wrappers flap down the street
dog poo sticks to the cracks in your feet
weed killer soaks through the gaps in the soil
thousands destroyed by one spillage of oil.
Spraying toxins on their grapes
breeding pets in funny shapes
pumping sewage out to sea.
Doesn't seem too bright to me.

They poison themselves, the land, the seed
and plunder all else in a frenzy of greed
they scatter their litter without any shame
yet they moan about rats as though we're to blame.

The System Stinks

'The system stinks', grumbles Gran,
   banging her newspaper with a knobbly fist.
'Not in front of the lad', dad hissed.
'What's the system, Gran?'

'It's half the world poor and with little to eat
while the rich just get fatter on burgers and sweets
~ look at this kid with no shoes on her feet'.

'The system stinks,' growls Gran,
turning the pages in her straight-backed chair.
'Give it a rest', snaps dad with a glare.
'What's the system, Gran?'

'It's the food you see on the shelves in the shop
processed and packaged from a poor farmer's crop
~ deeper in poverty with every price drop'.

'The system stinks', spits Gran,
tossing her paper on the threadbare rug.
Dad gives an angry, impatient shrug.
'What's the system, Gran?'

'It's the terms of trade that let rich people get
cheap products, cheap labour – blood, tears and sweat
~ then they give to charity and think they've paid their
debt'.

'The system stinks', shouts Gran,
sipping her tea that's gone cold by her side.

Dad brushes passed with an irritated sigh ~
'if they worked a bit harder I'm sure they'd survive'.
'What's the system, Gran?'

'It's this bleeding country with no sense of shame,
turning its back and doling out blame ~
but we're all tied up in this bloodthirsty game'.

'The system stinks', thunders Gran.
She pulls herself up with a wincing groan.
Dad clatters off to answer the phone.

I hear how his voice changes in tone.
Then he stands shocked in the hall
'they're closing the works – we've all lost our jobs'
he places the telephone back on the wall
'to somewhere they'll make a few extra bob'
then he roars and he stamps so my head starts to
throb.

'The system stinks', bellows dad – 'd'you hear that,
lad?'
but he crumples and drowns in a wellful of sobs
and he curls like a child in his mother's arms
where he looks like a boy all fragile and thin.
'We'll fight it', says Gran, 'we'll fight till we win'.

Blood in the Grass

It looked like a toy, left there in the grass
something to show to the rest of the class.
I bent down to touch it
and heard someone scream.
They said it was me.

Blood in the grass
blood in my dreams
nothing is ever quite what it seems.

I'd strayed from the path on my way to the spring
where the crystals of water chatter and sing
and there in the grass was a spherical dome
five steel prongs and a strip of wire.

Just as it triggered
I remembered the rule
the pictures
the warnings they gave us at school.
With a shrilling squeal it flew in the air
and spat steel splinters
everywhere.

Blood in the grass
blood in my face.

And then the screaming really starts
I hear my sister whoop and yelp
her panic as she runs to help.
I try to stop her with a shout

but only groans and grunts
spew out.
She calls my name in frightened pain,
and then
I hear it all again
the whizzing sounds, it bounds up high.
Bang!
Shards of metal fill the sky.

Hollow silence.
Scattered scars - a legacy of hate.

Blood in the grass
blood in my dreams
seeds of horror
a harvest of screams.

A Hunt for Wisdom

after Market Square *by A.A.Milne*

I had a penny,
a bright new penny,
I took my penny to university.
I wanted some wisdom,
some clever, learned wisdom
and I looked for some wisdom
'most everywhere.

I went to the college where they teach philosophy,
("only seven grand for a degree in philosophy!")
"Have you got some wisdom, 'cos I don't like
philosophy?"
But they hadn't any wisdom, not anywhere there.

I had a penny,
and I had another penny.
I took my pennies to God's house of prayer.
I did want some wisdom
a wealth of ancient wisdom,
and I looked for some wisdom
'most everywhere.

And I went to the altar where they sell you eternity,
("give your soul now and you're guaranteed eternity!")
"Have you got some wisdom, 'cos I don't want
eternity?"
But they hadn't any wisdom, not anywhere there.

I found a sixpence
a little white sixpence.
I took it in my hand
to Parliament Square.
I was buying my wisdom
(I do like wisdom)
and I looked for my wisdom
'most everywhere.

So I went to the hustings where they sold false
promises,
("give us your vote and you'll get false promises!")
"Could I have some wisdom 'cos I've had enough of
promises?".
But they hadn't any wisdom, not anywhere there.

I had nuffin'
no, I hadn't got nuffin'.
So I didn't bother hunting
for my wisdom anywhere.
But I walked through the village
the hustling, bustling village
and I saw lots of wisdom
'most everywhere.

So I'm sorry for the lecturers who teach you
philosophy,
I'm sorry for the ministers who offer you eternity
and I'm sorry for the government who try to run the
country
'cos they haven't any wisdom, not anywhere there.

Gene Genie

When you're cutting up the genes in a set of DNA
and you're so engrossed in progress that you
can't hear people say
'just be careful what you're splicing or you'll ruin nature's way'
have a think about the price that the world will have to
pay.

Roses that glow when you water them well
onions that grow with a beautiful smell
oysters with bracelets of pearls in their shell
hair that will shape without oodles of gel.

When you claim you're making miracles to feed the
starving poor
and you think the world will never see a famine any
more
are you sure about the motives of the boss you're working for?
as it's money makes the world go round and opens
nature's door.

Apples that kill every maggot in sight
hens that lay eggs without needing the light
people that work every day and all night
that have no need for sleep and eat less than a bite.

When you sell a farmer seeds that will never reproduce
and you patent genes of foodstuff that has been in
constant use

and you make her buy your pesticides or fine her for misuse
you've a greater chance, among the poor, of tightening the noose.

Salmon that swell up to five times their size
pigs that are bred without mouths, ears or eyes
medicine spliced into tropical flies
cocktails of pets for the wealthier guys.

If you'd like to make designer food that runs around your plate
and a brand new face and body that you think you'll never hate
are you mindful of the changes that these luxuries dictate
and the side effects and poverty they're likely to create?

Ready-skinned lambs that you eat when they're raw
dogs that are styled to have no bottom jaw
cows with no legs that spray milk from the floor
and men designed solely as fodder for war.

So you understand the code in a set of DNA
you've got the genie out now and you're gearing up to play
but before you have your bit of fun, just hear what people say
'have a think about the price that the world will have to pay.'

That Noble Heart

She had a noble heart
a beneficent, benevolent, humanitarian heart,
so I thought at the start, a heart of gold.
And rich pickings for me.

She wanted infants, orphans, waifs and strays;
poor, victims of war
those with no scope, whose parents can't cope.
'Smuggle them here for a new start in life', she said
and the American dream rolled on in my head.

The dollars poured recklessly onto my plate;
hundreds of children crawled into the States
to that selfless, virtuous, magnanimous heart
for a new start.

I suffocated signs of the untoward:
the shadow tugging at my shirt
the haunting pleas that called from the trees,
a mournful song, a wail, a moan
I'd turn to look but find I was all alone.

But now in my head I hear the hubbub
the clattering of knives
the scarring screams that pierce the farthest star
and fear that rips the pale moon's face apart.

Too late I discovered the depth of that heart,
that dog-eaten, rat-infested, hell-hag's heart,
that half-chewed, putrid, fool's gold heart.

I retched and puked till my guts stuck in my throat
I sicked and spewed at the sight
of clamps and tongs and eyes on stalks
livers and kidneys and tiny hearts still beating
extracted and labelled for her magnificent scheme:
spare parts for the American dream.

Coke

You've seen the ad, the sexy bloke,
oppressive heat, the can of coke.
Ice cubes crack, glasses chink.
All life's magic, in one drink.

I know it's just the advertiser's marketing device
an effective kind of show for them to lever up the price
by making people think that it's the way to paradise
while their eyes are on the profits and their own enormous
slice.

Semi-naked, beads of sweat.
Peeping girls, he's never met.
Cold can pops, ice cubes fizz
the coolest, wettest, drink there is.

And though I always thought the ad a silly sort of joke
it seems I've been persuaded by the Coca Cola folk:
I was stranded in a jungle with a hot and sexy bloke
and the only thing I fancied was an ice-cold can of coke.

Girl emerges, warm eyes meet
coke cools down, the passionate heat.
Warm lips part, tongues are wet.
Enjoy Coca Cola, the best you'll get.

But I'm always disappointed when I've drunk a glass or two.
It never seems to do exactly what it's meant to do,
like the mirage in the desert, like the seed that never grew,
like a father's empty promise or a dream that won't come true.

peach wine & toffee apples

Bills and Moon

When the book you've bought is battered but it didn't cost a lot,
and the hooks have all been shattered 'cos the blurb tells all the plot,
and you look for idle chatter 'cos your brain's tied in a knot,
you're a shattered, battered, chatterbox whose brain has lost the plot.

Well, it's better than a natter on a Sunday afternoon,
and the bit of blurb is splattered with a saucy, sexy swoon,
and you think it doesn't matter that the author's a baboon,
you're a shattered, knackered slacker with the latest Mills and Boon.

When the girl is very pretty but is shy and all alone,
there's an earl who's dark and gritty, or a guy who's made of stone,
and the pearl that's in his kitty is a huge testosterone,
it's a bit of nitty gritty with a moral undertone.

When the heroine is crying 'cos she's made a big mistake,
and she's very close to dying from the venom of a snake,
but the hairy man comes flying with his juicy pound of steak,
it's a wary scary subtext where your dignity's at stake.

When your reading is exceeding all the other things
you do,
and you're pleading with your library to import a ton
or two,
and you're reading while you're breeding and
proceeding to be needing the stampeding of a hero
who can cock-a-doodle-do....
then...

you're a pretty, gritty kitty with a stamina of iron,
eating buttered, battered booklets with the hunger of a
lion,
you'll impress the best assessor from the moon to
Cameroon

by your cluttered, clattered
chuttered, chattered
knickered, knackered
shickered shackered
brickered, brackered
tittered, tattered
notes on Mills and Boon.

No more *Old Maid*

When my neighbour left the country, I was
worried who'd move in,
but the council found a tenant who was young and
neat and slim.
The other neighbours called the girl *a useless piece of
scum,*
but I don't have a problem with her being a single
mum.

It wasn't long before she knocked and hovered at my
door,
her daughter and a battered teddy sprawled across the
floor.
She said, 'I've no hot water. Could you fill my thermos
flask?'
and I'm pleased she had the confidence to feel that she
could ask.

She came round every day, I'd say, for tea or milk or
bread.
'Feel free to ask for anything, my dear,' I always said.
For, though I'm old and others say I'm rather highly
strung,
I know that in this era, it's not easy being young.

So then she called and asked me, in a manner still
polite
'Can I borrow your virginity on Saturday night?'
I stared at her in horror – you could hear my curlers
pop.

A cup of sugar's one thing, but I do know where to stop.

But then I thought, I'm being selfish. Goodness gracious me,
I haven't got much use for it - I'm nearly eighty-three.
I've kept it trim and proper since I came onto this earth.
Just imagine what the blasted thing would probably be worth.

'You'd best come in', I chirruped, 'I shall get it out and packed,
but I'm really quite attached to it – I have to have it back.'
Her eyes lit up in wonder when she saw it on the tray.
'It's the best I've ever seen', she gasped. It really made my day.

I wished her luck and sent her off into the dying light
and I stayed awake all fluttery on Saturday night.
She popped it back on Sunday in her dressing gown and socks
it was shoved all numb and floppy in a Tupperware box.

I tell you, I was saddened till I put it back inside
and then I felt a kind of rush, a blush of beaming pride.
It's almost like divinity is all around the place
and I just can't seem to wipe this wretched smile from

off my face!

Well now we're best of friends, you know – we laugh
and play such games
and the neighbours never trouble us or call us silly
names.
I've always thought there'd be less war and conflict
everywhere
if all the people in the world would only learn to share.

Position Vacant: Creative Writer

Thanks for coming, take a pew.
We're glad you could make the interview
Joyce and me and James and Sue will make the final
choice.

We've read your form while drinking tea
were exhausted by page seventy
but that's enough for now from me.
First question now, please Joyce.

Do you ever fantasize, imagine, dream or otherwise
allow yourself to compromise the realities of life?
Do you live in other worlds with desert gold and deep-
sea pearls
where minotaurs eat boys and girls or a gorilla takes a
wife?

I did, with reservation, put on my application
my rosemary extension which keeps Jabberwocks away
my house is quite a busy spot, with goblins, elves and God
knows what,
and women in the attic who are screaming night and day.

Do you choose your clothes with care and grope to see
if Narnia's there?
On mornings when you brush your hair is Alice
through the glass?
D'you enjoy imagination while you're waiting at the
station
and erotic fascination if you stare at someone's arse?

I allowed myself the liberty of listing on my gold CV
the plastic suits I model and the helmets I design.
I make love on the railway tracks to businessmen, compu-
ter hacks
and First Great Western porters as they're knocking back
the wine.

Do you hike the galaxy while sipping at your morning
tea,
the daily news read heedlessly from the radio on the
wall?
Does your hamster talk to you? Do your kids live in a
shoe?
Do you think your world is true or d'you fabricate it
all?

I travel most by hovercraft unless I'm feeling really daft
when I'll hire a public toilet which can fly above the land.
If I'm late I simply say a ghost was standing in my way.
It usually does the business and my friends all understand.

You fit all our criteria
You suffer from deliria
and probably hysteria
I'll say that, if I may?

We are all impressed with you.
The job is yours. Please take it, do.
I'd love a lift home in your loo, if you've got it here
today.

****

The queue is getting shorter and a sweet placates my daughter
but the weather's pretty rotten as I sign on for my dole.
I am insane, or so it seems, but what is life without our dreams?
My world is full of fantasy - it brightens up my soul.

Hyperactive Knickers

I once knew a pair of hyperactive knickers
they were red silky satin ones
with bows and frills and lace
and they danced to the tune of a pop-up *Karma Sutra*
and they'd flirt with all the boxer shorts
in every public place.

And after several years of finny fannying about
the satin started thinning
and the bows began to fray
and they met a pair of wyefronts that were baggy at the
bottom
and they settled in a drawer
and just came out on Christmas Day.

The lace became all stiff and the elastic started sagging
but they didn't let that stop them
finding time to misbehave
and it wasn't till the moths had eaten almost every
scrap
that the hyperactive knickers
went kicking to the grave.

Barbie's Boobies

Barbie's got boobies
like right royal rubies
big bulbous bosoms
the hue of fresh dewb'ries.
Barbie's got boobies
big whopping g'noobies
pink plastic doobies
like tupperware jugs.
Genetically modified
tucked and trimmed boobies
extended and swollen
with dubious drugs.
Barbie's got boobies
like right royal rubies
Barbie's got boobies
like pink plastic jugs.

Which God?

Do you feel suicidal? Are you fed up with your wife?
D'you ever think you need a bit of faith within your
life?
Are you flummoxed by the massive range of gods upon
the scene?
Well – have a read of this month's *Which? Consumer
Magazine.*

Our team of experts really put religion to the test,
reviewing all the major gods and judging which is best.
Assessing sacred substance and the price you'll have to
pay,
our panel found a deity that won in every way.

The favoured faith is 'shopping' – it is worshipped
everywhere.
We found that direct purchase is more practical than
prayer.
For spiritual experience, or when you're feeling blue
there's nothing that a touch of retail therapy can't do.

You can meditate on glitter to enhance your
fingernails.
You can reach your own nirvana in the January sales.
Every shop is kosher, and there's no such place as hell
and ritual means a damn good shop and chocolate
cake as well.

No need to give up luxuries. No karma, sin or guilt.
No need to hide the signs of any seed you might have

spilt.

No need to lop your foreskin, or lie prostrate on the floor

and the only place to pilgrim is the factory outlet store.

So hit the road of sanctity with visa card and pen.

Go forth and shop and tell the world of being born again.

But don't forget your bible, for without it you're unclean.

Subscribe today to *Which? The only sacred magazine.*

Consultation Caper in Poets' Corner

*Could you please be seated now, the Dean is going
spare.*
*The Abbey, as you all well know, is still a house of prayer
and tourists often get alarmed when things are out of
place.*
*So, poets, could you please sit down? - there should be
ample space.*

*I'd like to introduce myself, my name is Martha Barts
I've taken up a contract in Westminster Borough Arts.
I'd like to get your thoughts on making poetry attractive -
it could be intellectual, it could be interactive.*

*This project that I'm working on will need some expert
steering -*
'Could you please speak up a bit, I'm rather hard of
hearing?'
'She said she's got some project on. Just listen for a
change!'
'Well, talking to a bunch of ghosts just seems a little
strange'.

'The Council's got some funding now, from Camelot I
think.'
'Oh cursèd be that wretched place, I'd rather have a
drink!'
'I think you'll find that getting sense from Blake will
be a bore.
He only speaks to fairies now who waltz across the
floor.'

'O come, come lads, let's show the lass a wee bit o'
respect.
It sounds as though our poems too ha' gone into
neglect.
Let's gi' her what she wants to know and ha' a drop o'
wine.
Let's hold our hands together for the sake of Auld Lang
Syne.'

'Well, my advice is just to wander lonely as a cloud,
and as you go, just let it flow - just say the words out
loud.'
'That's too much walking, Wordsworth man, you need
your strength of mind,
and get to grips with things that drive the whole of
humankind.'

'I quite agree. Why ever write about a Nightingale?'
'Well, why would people read about your days in
Reading Gaol?'
'There's more to life than mellow mists and sumptuous
Autumn yields.'
'You need to speak of Light Brigades and bloody
battlefields.'

'Martha, please, ignore this lot, they're far too out of
date.
Just get yourself a pea-green boat and find a feathered
mate.
Retreat to somewhere magical and dance beneath the
moon.'

'Oh get your nonsense out of here! Incompetent baboon!'

'I worry for your flock, poor dab, and warn you of the night.
Do not go gentle, Martha, in the dying of the light.'
'Oh, come now Dylan, silence is the poet's cornerstone.
Stop all the clocks, is my advice and cut the telephone.'

'Well Martha, if you keep your head with all these poets fighting,
you're strong enough to face the world and leave them to their writing.'
But what about my project and the poet consultation?
I've got to put your comments in my monthly presentation.

'Well here's our thoughts. Now write them down, and pass them on, my dear,
we're sick of blinking poetry - it's all we ever hear.
And I'm convinced that if we men had not already died,
by now, for sure, we would have all committed suicide.'

The Grand Fiction Ball

They came in their droves on that warm summer's
    night,
their language like crystals in shimmering light.
Their rhythms and rhymes were a wordsmith's delight
as they flocked to the Grand Fiction Ball.

The queue went down fast as they paid to go in,
the sonnets, short stories, a yarn in a spin,
a crowd of biographies drinking sloe gin,
the nursery rhymes wrapped in a shawl.

A novel stood shyly a glass in his hand.
He'd never set foot in a place quite so grand,
mixing with words he did not understand,
and he gazed all around in delight.

He watched as a tongue-twister chattered away,
and the riddles make fun of a couplet at play,
and he laughed when some nonsense arrived on a tray
that was soaring up high like a kite.

A haiku sailed passed him, so dainty and slight
her words so compact and her meaning so tight.
She swanned passed the food and took less than a bite,
and she boasted with pride of her diet.

An autobiography strode passed the stage
with an arrogant look and a flick of his page.
A buzz of biographies asked him his age
but his sarcasm made them go quiet.

A limerick joked of an innocent bride.
The novel went over and laughed till he cried,
but a very old ballad took him aside
and rambled on into the night.

The novel, while collared by such a great bore,
then spotted a poem walk in through the door.
Her words were flamboyant with symbols galore
and he knew it was love at first sight.

He stared in amazement and squirmed in his seat.
Her metaphors rocked as she swayed to the beat
he truly believed that his joy was complete
when she came up and asked him to dance.

They jived and they salsad with expert gyration.
He gently caressed her personification.
She laughed when he showed her his justification.
He swooned in a love-smitten trance.

They nestled while sharing a vodka and lime.
The poem spoke softly in delicate rhyme,
hyperbole's fluttering all of the time.
She seductively touched chapter four.

Their passion went forth at a rollicking pace,
exciting each comma, each hyphen, each space.
They linked up their words in romantic embrace,
and happily lived ever more.

Techno-trouble

Oh, Mr. Jacob! It's your answerphone again,
and my time machine has broken and it's filling
up with rain.
Your guarantee informs me you'll respond to every call,
but when I try to contact you there's no-one there at
all.

You see, Mr. Jacob, there's a dial that's gone off track,
and I've sent my four researchers off but now can't get
them back.
To make it worse their mums are pacing round my
sitting room
and they've threatened to castrate me if their kids are
not back soon.

I followed your instructions when I sent them off in
May.
They reached their destination times within the nearest
day.
They're spread across the centuries now with data
logging pages
to gauge how English literature has grown throughout
the ages.

But now, Mr. Jacob, can you tell me what to do?
I'm scared of being pounced on as I come out of the
loo.
I can hear the knives a-sharpening and women's
wicked calls.
I've locked and chained the toilet door. I'm clutching

both my balls!

Can I, Mr. Jacob, can I tell them where they are?
Little Jenny's in sixth century at some Anglo-Saxon
bar.
She's found a poem called Beowulf which she read
while drinking stout.
But it's all about the Danes and so she chucked the
damn thing out.

And James is not much better when it comes to
observation.
He seems to think the Wife of Bath is waiting at the
station.
How can any history student with the tiniest of brain
think that Chaucer and his motley crew were
pilgrimming by train?

There's Tommy who is drinking all his wages now, I
bet.
I asked him to involve himself with all the Bloomsbury
set.
He's on some inner journey like some stuck up little
twit,
and the data that he's sending through's a useless pile
of shit.

I'm feeling rather sorry though for Mrs. Taylor's
daughter
who spends her time at Shelley's house in buckets full
of water.

And Percy Bysshe administers a twenty-voltage shock ~
But the data makes it all worthwhile for turning back
the clock.

To be honest, Mr. Jacob, I'd rather let them go.
Well, they're not the best researchers in the world as
you well know.
But my balls are very dear to me and just the thought
of pain
gives me all the more incentive now to get them back
again.

The walls are shaking visibly, they're kicking down the
door.
Mr. Jacob answer quickly for I can't hold on much
more!
They're poking me with wires from your stupid time
machine.
And they're pressing all the buttons now - why can't
you intervene?!

****

Oh Mr. Jacob, this is all so very weird.
My house has been extended and I've grown a bushy
beard.
I must be in the future! Phew! I'm saved from fiendish
squalls!
I like it here. I think I'll stay. But shit! I've got no balls!

Instant Satisfaction for 99p

Do you long for action?
For instant satisfaction?
A yearning for learning or idle distraction?

Brought to you
new. From the makers of *literature shakers*
poetry capsules, sachets of song.

Pot Fiction. Total sensation.
Just add water and steep for five minutes.

Feed your mind. Free your soul.
Smell, taste, hear, touch, see.
All for 99p.

Hundreds of flavours; all the old favourites,
contemporary fiction, subversive rhyme.
Something for all, for every occasion
in any location, at any time.

Pop it in your handbag. Slip one to a friend. Enjoy
every minute you spend.

Organic, fresh, hand-selected. GM-free.

Easy to make. An excellent choice.
Money-back guarantee.
Pot Fiction
Instant satisfaction
for just 99p.

blood orange & crystallised ginger

Screaming to a Halt

When life presents nuggets,
         unexpected, unexplained bargains
that lift my step
that little bit higher;

when I plunge my hands into
time's darkness
and touch reflections of my phantasies
in liquid gold reality
I clutch
the memory and grin
at strangers.

But out of the elated mass
of gyrating brain cells
there is one – always one –
that sticks its head above the crowd
and points and jeers
and sneers in mocking screech,
leaching poisoned hate
and deflating delight
far
far into the night.

The Lot of the Lazy Bee

In Welsh, the male bee
is called
the lazy bee;
explanation unnecessary.

He hangs around the hive
with large eyes and
hairy back.

On sunny days
he flies to meet his friends
and sniff the breeze
for a whiff
of a queen.

As the sun dips to its
winter course,
the hive is cleared
of unnecessary baggage.
All males are dragged
and dumped
outside to perish
or be pecked up
by a grateful
robin.

The Clever Marketing of Honey

Worker bees have a special
tummy
for transporting nectar.

They lick and suck and slurp
the golden juice.
They gulp and swallow and burp
and carry it home

where
it is regurgitated
and stored in wax comb.

It was a wise old bird
who coined the word
honey.
For, I suspect
'local, organic bee sick'
might not sell
quite so well.

Egg Machine

In the hot summer throes,
when the scented flower grows
and the sweet nectar flows
a queen bee
lays
about two thousand eggs
every day.

She's licked
and fed
and
pampered
and
nursed
and guided and
manoeuvred and
directed and dictated and
restricted and constricted.

Her life is simply to lay
about two thousand
eggs
every day.

Poetic Madness: come buy, come buy

I've often heard it said
that a good poet's sanity is very thinly spread
they tread at the edge where reason starts to shred
dreaded delusions and illusions of the dead.
Balanced at the brink like Blake or Byron
a siren seducing a mottled mind
'mad as the winds'
blown off course by fanatical imaginings.

I longed for a touch of that half-crazed fertility
a spoonful, a sprinkle, a splash of that insanity
a tipple, a trickle to spur my creativity
to pour from my veins in a frenzied flood:
imagination dusted with dried Bedlam blood.

So I clutched fifty quid
I consulted a quack
I said 'all the best poets were slightly mad
I'll have a little bit of whatever they had'
and boy was he a crack!
Took me to the womb and back
poked at bits of my brain
that had never seen the light of day:
subconscious phantasies of self-annihilation
frenzied fixations with reincarnation
obvious, he stated, by my constipation;
repressed,
self-obsessed
a warped hankering for the opposite sex

and still not divest
of my *Oedipal Complex.*

I flew from the room at the end of the session
a feral fire of premenstrual aggression
'this is it' I roared
wild as a wuthering moor
shaking a Shelleyed fist to the world.
I picked up my pen and prepared for the poetry
to pour on the page.

But I waited and waited
sated with simmering anguish
that ticked in an unhinged rhythm
pen poised
but every noise
rippled the waters
of the stagnant void below
where tears are stored but never flow.

Not a line, a word, no rhyme
could shake the gloom
consuming every breath
just signs that pointed the road to death.

I crawled back to the couch and lay
so much on my mind yet so little to say
'you'll need five years - a session a day'
and he smiled
'now - how would you like to pay?'

The Scrap

I bump into Sheila down at Tesco's
limping and lopsided.
Hasn't changed though – not a scrap.
Still flares her nostrils to the sky -
trying not to breathe the air the rest of us have used.

Hello Sheila, I chirp, *remember me?*
from university.
[You used to say I had an ugly face,
and spread rumours about me all over the place.]

Oh! Empty smile and grated laugh, *how*
lovely to see you!

That's an awful limp, I say
toe obstructing the wheel of her trolley.
Malcolm crashed the car and crushed my leg
it's never been right since.

But Sheila, I quiz, *haven't you been down the scrap yard;*
the body recycling?
Hmm? her ears wriggle with interest - never did get my
jokes.
So I carry on
You could pick up another leg, easy
save you hopping around on those old pins.

And though she's hoity toity, I know she wants more.
They've got some lovely bits and bobs there
it needs a wash but it scrubs up good as new.

And I touch my face,
New cheeks last year - no wrinkles, see
that's probably why you didn't recognise me.

I bite my lip and on I go,
I've got an account with the Scrap
Oh, I'm always popping in for this or that.
There's a sale on legs at the moment:
two for the price of one - you can't go wrong.
And fingers by the check-out, just like sweeties.

Her eyes are dancing all over my body
she touches my arm and looks me in the eye,
I do remember you, her voice soft as a marshmallow
you did well – top of the class.

There is a quiver in her lip
will you take me? Show me how it works
She draws me closer to the meat counter
it's Malcolm, you see – he wants a younger model.

And I say, *sorry Sheila, I've got shopping to do*
I pick up a packet of sausages and smartly walk away
I don't know why - I never eat meat.

Buried Treasure

Brambling hate
swarms across virgin fields
thrusting twisted thorns into soft flesh
of once-precious love,
distorting memories
shredding dignity
churning intimacy into clawed meat.
Like vomit from a feast.

And you,
you that once dangled and swung
across dirty puddles and cracked pavements
a laughing bundle gripped by two giant hands.
The link in a chain of magic.
Essence of life
epitome of love.

Now
stuck in the middle
in a mad, muddled match
of bitterness
of back-stabbing, blood-shot jealousy
sapping, sucking, slithering
in the rotten muck, hoof-trodden
ankle-deep shit.

A go-between
ferrying from headland to pier
in stagnant water
where tankers of resent

have spilt their acid jewels
across midnight whispers
dawn desires
blind, bewitched belief.

You
running messages
in your frail dinghy
unstable, unsettled
reeling, rolling, rocking.
The link in a chain of destruction
the pawn in a game of deceit.

Suffocating screams of self-identity
squeezed from a thousand veins.
Numbed pain
again
and again
until, like buried treasure
under a lonely island
and waves of daily death
it lies dormant
waiting,
waiting for the moment to re-emerge.

Tattooed Goddess

Picking through the carcass of a dream
scraps of sinews hang
as loose strands in a story
mis-spelled, half-formed
spoilt, spent actors in a show
that never played
a joke that never laughed
a word that never spoke.

Not a choke
nor a spaced-out wise-crack
but guised, selected lies.
A cushion with no filling
a life without living.

Stretched and strung upon a rack
a teased thread
hooked on conscience and jealous guilt.
Shaved
planed
tidied
boxed
packaged to fit with the rest of the world.

No.
Lick the rules from the blackboard
spit the social code on the streets
of prejudice
and power and threat
spin the feathered flocks into a calypso

a jackpot
a Russian roulette.
Pounce on the present with greedy
lucky-dip hands
crush convention in a vice of life
and
like a tattooed goddess
gorge from a chalice of wet pleasure.

Surf the sunspots, surging, splashing, crashing
wading through white light
dragging the glow, the molten heat
the burning core
into your veins
Burn. Love.
Live.

The Thing in the Jar on my Window Sill.

With tuppence, I tighten a virgin blade
slice through the centre of my scalp
neat hole drilled into toughened skull.

I poke my fingers in
to the frenzied chaos of whirling words that
flash and dart
in clashing colour.
Fluorescent images, iridescent silhouettes.

Fingers rummage through soft flesh
electric pulses flit and jolt
strands of memory
slip through my hand
as I sift among
scolding thoughts and
hardened dreams gone cold.

Buried under layers of contorted behaviour
and mis-said words,
I feel the grain, the pain.
A gristled nugget jelled
into a nutshell of tension.

With tweezers
I remove its irritation.